Dinosaurs

Published by Hinkler Pty Ltd
45–55 Fairchild Street
Heatherton Victoria 3202 Australia
www.hinkler.com

© Hinkler Pty Ltd 2021

Design and illustrations: Dynamo Design
Cover design: Mandy Norman

ISBN: 978 1 8651 5205 9

Printed and bound in China

CONTENTS

Dinosaurs 2
  Dinosaur families 2
  A changing earth 3
  The evolution of dinosaurs 3
Triassic period 4
Jurassic period 6
Laurasia 6
  North America 6
  Europe 6
  Asia 6
  Gondwana 7
  South America 7
  Africa 7
Cretaceous period 8
  North America 8
  Europe 9
  Asia 9
  South America 10
  Africa 10
  Oceania 10
Extinction 11
Glossary 12
Dinosaur world map 47
Conclusion 48

hinkler

DINOSAURS

Dinosaurs were powerful prehistoric animals that lived on Earth for 160 million years, before suddenly becoming extinct 65 million years ago.

Dinosaurs were scaly, egg-laying reptiles, resembling the crocodiles or lizards of today. Dinosaurs included herbivores (plant-eaters) and carnivores (meat-eaters). Some dinosaurs stood on all fours (quadrupeds), while others were bipedal, standing on their two back legs.

Everything we know about dinosaurs comes from fossil remains such as

bones, teeth and claws, which were buried and turned to stone over time.

Dinosaur scales have been found, but as all fossils are stone-coloured, it is impossible to tell what colour dinosaurs were.

DINOSAUR FAMILIES

Dinosaurs are divided into two groups, saurischia *(saw-RISK-ee-a)* and ornithischia *(OR-ni-THISK-ee-a)*. The groups are distinguished by pelvis shape. Saurischians were 'lizard-hipped', while the ornithischians were 'bird-hipped'.

The saurischian group was made up of theropods and sauropods. Theropods were fast and ferocious bipedal

carnivores. They included Tyrannosaurus *(ti-RAN-o-SAWR-us)*.

Sauropods were large, long-necked herbivores. They included Diplodocus *(di-PLOD-o-kus)*.

The ornithischian group was made up of all the remaining dinosaurs. Some stood on two legs and some stood on four. Many of them had plates, armour, horns or spikes to protect them from predators.

Saurischia: theropods

Saurischia: sauropods

Ornithischia

A CHANGING EARTH

Since the formation of the earth, many plants and creatures have evolved and died out. Dinosaurs lived in the Triassic, Jurassic and Cretaceous periods. The first modern humans evolved less than 2 million years ago, in the Quaternary period, which we live in now.

During the time when dinosaurs ruled the world, the earth went through many changes. During the Triassic period, all the continents were joined together in one land mass we call Pangaea. The land started breaking apart and drifting during the Jurassic and Cretaceous periods, eventually dividing the earth into continents.

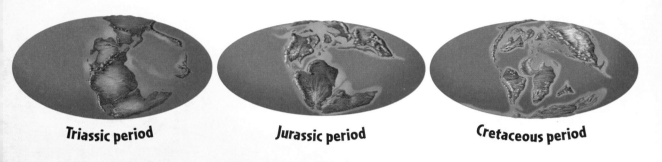

Triassic period   Jurassic period   Cretaceous period

THE EVOLUTION OF DINOSAURS

The first creatures to live on Earth inhabited the ocean. They were simple organisms such as seaweed, jellyfish and shellfish. Eventually there came to be fish, land plants, insects, amphibians and reptiles.

Before the coming of the dinosaurs, Earth was inhabited by prehistoric creatures, including massive reptiles.

Unlike most reptiles, dinosaurs stood on upright legs that were located straight under their bodies. Other reptiles, including lizards, had bent legs that came out of the sides of their bodies.

Legs of a dinosaur

Modern-day lizard

TRIASSIC PERIOD

The Triassic period extended from about 250 to 200 million years ago. The earth was not divided into continents then as it is today, but was all one supercontinent that we call Pangaea, surrounded by an ocean we call Panthalassa.

The climate of the earth at this time was hot and dry. There was hardly any life on the land during the early Triassic period, with living things mainly occupying marine environments.

Eventually, marine creatures started to inhabit the land, and it is possible that dinosaurs evolved from these prehistoric reptilians.

Some of the earliest dinosaurs appeared in the mid to late Triassic period.

They included Coelophysis (*SEEL-o-FIE-sis*), a slender theropod that lived in North America.

It is possible that Coelophysis lived in packs, as many fossils of this dinosaur have been found together at Ghost Ranch in New Mexico.

A flock of Coelophysis

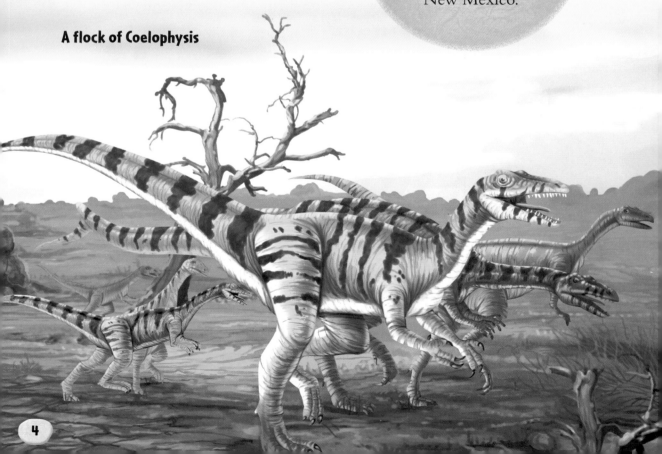

Late Triassic dinosaurs in the European region included the large plant-eating Plateosaurus *(PLAT-ee-o-SAWR-us)* and Liliensternus *(LIL-ee-en-SHTER-nus)*, a small and speedy carnivore.

Pisanosaurus *(pee-SAHN-o-SAWR-us)* was an ornithischian plant-eater found in South America. It was hunted by Herrerasaurus *(he-RER-a-SAWR-us)*, a small, fast and sharp-toothed theropod.

During the late Triassic period, as the first dinosaurs were evolving on the land, pterosaurs *(TER-o-sawrs)*, the largest flying creatures of all time, inhabited the skies. Pterosaurs were not actually dinosaurs, but massive winged reptiles.

The exact appearance of Liliensternus is unknown — it might have been covered in scales or feathers.

Scaled Liliensternus

Feathered Liliensternus

Herrerasaurus hunting Pisanosaurus

JURASSIC PERIOD

The Jurassic period took place around 199 to 145 million years ago. During the early Jurassic period, Pangaea broke up into two supercontinents: Laurasia to the north and Gondwana to the south.

The climate on Earth was warm and wet, providing vegetation and allowing dinosaurs to thrive. Dinosaurs became larger and many more species evolved.

LAURASIA

In Laurasia, there was an abundance of plants and many plant-eating dinosaurs, which meant that theropod predators had plenty of prey.

NORTH AMERICA

Jurassic North America was home to many dinosaurs. Allosaurus *(AL-o-SAWR-us)* was a frightening theropod — a massive meat-eater reaching about 10 metres (33 feet) in height.

There were also giant sauropods such as Apatosaurus *(a-PAT-o-SAWR-us)*, Camarasaurus *(KAM-a-ra-SAWR-us)* and Diplodocus *(di-PLOD-o-kus)*, some of the biggest dinosaurs that ever existed.

It is estimated that Diplodocus reached around 27 metres (88.5 feet) in length.

EUROPE

In Europe, a 9-metre-long (30-foot) carnivore called Megalosaurus *(MEG-a-lo-SAWR-us)* reigned.

The late Jurassic period in Europe was also home to what scientists think was the first ever bird, Archaeopteryx *(AHR-kee-OP-ter-iks)*.

ASIA

Asia was home to Yangchuanosaurus *(YAHNG-chwahn-o-SAWR-us)*, a horned theropod that preyed on sauropods including Mamenchisaurus *(mah-MUHN-chee-SAWR-us)* and Omeisaurus *(UH-may-SAWR-us)*, as well as ornithiscian stegosaurs.

Stegosaurus

Apatosaurus

Allosaurus

GONDWANA

The new supercontinent of Gondwana was warm and flourishing, with plants providing plenty of food for animals, which were growing in size and number.

SOUTH AMERICA

Gondwana was home to large sauropods like the short–necked Brachytrachelopan (*BRAK-e-TRAK-o-LO-pan*). South America's sauropods continued growing and evolving, and by the Cretaceous period they were among the largest creatures to have ever walked the earth.

AFRICA

During the Jurassic period, massive dinosaurs appeared in Africa including the frightening theropod Ceratosaurus (*se-RAT-o-SAWR-us*), distinguishable by its horn, its massive jaws and predatory nature.

Kentrosaurus (*KEN-tro-SAWR-us*) was a stegosaurian similar to North America's Stegosaurus (*STEG-o-SAWR-us*). It was a spiky ornithischian living in the area of Tanzania, alongside massive sauropod Brachiosaurus (*BRAK-ee-o-SAWR-us*). Massospondylus (*ma-so-SPON-di-lus*) was a smallish, bipedal sauropod found in South Africa.

Dimorphodon

Megalosaurus

Chungkingosaurus

CRETACEOUS PERIOD

The Cretaceous period took place around 144 to 65 million years ago. During this time, the supercontinents of Laurasia and Gondwana broke up further, into the continents we have today.

Much of the land was covered by shallow water, and chalk rocks formed across the earth. The climate became cooler and seasons began. New life appeared, such as flowering plants, and with them, bees. Cretaceous Earth was also home to some of the first mammals and insects. The dinosaurs of the Cretaceous period were diverse and huge in size.

Quetzalcoatlus

Quetzalcoatlus, a flying reptile, had a wingspan of 12 metres (39 feet).

NORTH AMERICA

During the Cretaceous period, North America was divided into islands because of high water levels. It was full of vegetation and flowering plants, as well as tall trees. In the sky was Quetzalcoatlus (KWET-zal-ko-AT-lus), the largest being ever to fly.

North American sauropods began to die out in the Cretacean period and were replaced by horned dinosaurs and hadrosaurs — duck-billed dinosaurs.

Edmontosaurus (ed-MON-to-SAWR-us) was one of the largest hadrosaurs, measuring about 13 metres (43 feet) in length, and it cohabited with the hadrosaur Parasaurolophus (PAR-a-saw-ROL-o-fus), which had a large crest on its head.

Triceratops (trie-SER-a-tops) was a massive plant-eating ornithischian that used its frill and three sharp horns to protect itself from predators such as Deinonychus (die-NON-i-kus) and Tyrannosaurus (ti-RAN-o-SAWR-us).

Deinonychus was a small theropod that possibly hunted in packs, and used the sharp claws on its feet as powerful weapons against its prey. Tyrannosaurus was a fearsome hunter, with massive jaws and teeth that it used to tear and devour prey.

Tyrannosaurus

Parasaurolophus

Edmontosaurus

EUROPE

Like North America, much of Europe was covered by shallow seas, and most Cretacean dinosaurs lived on the tropical islands that remained above water.

Baryonyx *(BAR-ee-ON-iks)* was a large carnivore that used its sharp teeth and hooked claws for hunting marine animals.

Iguanodon *(i-GWAHN-o-don)* was a bulky herbivore that could stand on two legs or on four. Close relations of Iguanodon were the duck-billed hadrosaurs, including Telmatosaurus *(TEL-ma-to-SAWR-us)*.

Baryonyx hunting fish

Dsungaripterus

A Protoceratops and Velociraptor have been found fossilised in combat. Both dinosaurs died during the fight, probably due to a collapsing sand dune.

ASIA

Asia was the largest continent in the Cretaceous period and was home to many living creatures. Massive reptiles such as Dsungaripterus *(JUNG-gah-RIP-ter-us)* dominated the skies.

On the land was Gigantoraptor *(jig-ANT-o-RAP-tor)*, a large theropod that resembled a huge ostrich.

Saichania *(sie-KAHN-ee-a)* was bulky and armoured, equipped with a club-like tail. Protoceratops *(PROH-to-SER-a-tops)* was a horned plant-eater about the size of a sheep. Velociraptor *(vee-LOHS-i-RAP-tor)* was a small, fierce theropod.

Gigantoraptor

Protoceratops

Saichania

Velociraptor

SOUTH AMERICA

Saltasaurus *(SAHL-tah-SAWR-us)* and Rinconsaurus *(RIN-kon-SAWR-us)* were among the sauropods to inhabit Cretaceous South America. There was also Unenlagia *(oon-en-LAHG-ee-a)*, a strange-looking theropod whose name means 'halfbird'. Giganotosaurus *(jig-a-NOT-o-SAWR-us)* was a giant carnivore found in Argentina.

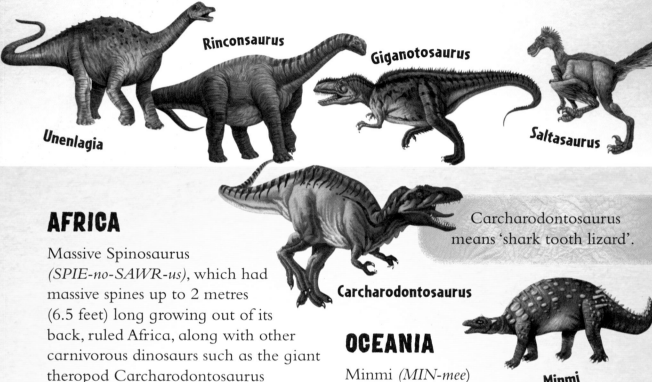

Rinconsaurus

Giganotosaurus

Unenlagia

Saltasaurus

Carcharodontosaurus means 'shark tooth lizard'.

Carcharodontosaurus

AFRICA

Massive Spinosaurus *(SPIE-no-SAWR-us)*, which had massive spines up to 2 metres (6.5 feet) long growing out of its back, ruled Africa, along with other carnivorous dinosaurs such as the giant theropod Carcharodontosaurus *(kahr-KAR-o-DON-to-SAWR-us)*, with its massive jaws and serrated teeth.

There was also Deltadromeus *(DEL-ta-DROHM-ee-us)*, another theropod giant, whose slender body shape and long limbs suggest it was a very fast runner.

OCEANIA

Minmi *(MIN-mee)* and Muttaburrasaurus *(muht-a-BUHR-a-SAWR-us)* were Australian dinosaurs found around Queensland. Muttaburrasaurus was an ornithopod and Minmi was a very small, armoured ankylosaur.

Minmi

Deltadromeus

Jobaria

Lurdusaurus

Muttaburrasaurus

EXTINCTION

All dinosaurs suddenly became extinct 65 million years ago, along with many other living creatures. This mass extinction is known as the Cretaceous–Tertiary extinction event.

There are several theories on why dinosaurs became extinct. Some scientists believe that it was due to the rapid change in atmosphere and climate that took place during the late Cretaceous period.

Others believe that Earth was hit by an asteroid or comet, which caused extreme temperatures that led to the extinction of most life on Earth.

Some believe that dinosaurs did not change their diet as the plant life changed, and so became extinct from lack of food.

The extinction event wiped out about three-quarters of life on Earth. Among the survivors were mammals. Much smaller than dinosaurs, these warm-blooded creatures were now free of the giant predators that had ruled Earth. Other survivors included the birds that now took over the sky, as the flying pterosaurs were all gone. Animals continued to evolve and diversify and eventually the earth became as it is today.

An icy Earth

GLOSSARY

Acrocanthosaurus (ak-roh-KANTH-uh-SAWR-us)

Meaning of name: high-spined lizard
Lived: 115–105 million years ago
Period: Cretaceous
Length: up to 12 m (40 ft)
Weight: about 2.3 t (2.5 US t, 2.3 UK t)
Diet: meat, including large plant-eating dinosaurs!
Location: North America (Canada, USA

Afrovenator (AF-roh-VEN-uh-tor)

Meaning of name: African hunter
Lived: 135–125 million years ago
Period: Cretaceous
Length: up to 9 m (30 ft)
Weight: about 1.4 t (1.5 US t, 1.4 UK t)
Diet: meat
Location: Africa (Niger)

Alamosaurus (AL-uh-moh-SAWR-us)

Meaning of name: Alamo lizard
Lived: 70–65 million years ago
Period: Cretaceous
Length: up to 21 m (70 ft)
Weight: about 27 t (30 US t, 27 UK t)
Diet: plants
Location: North America (USA)

Meaning of name: Alberta lizard
Lived: 76–74 million years ago
Period: Cretaceous
Length: up to 9 m (30 ft)
Weight: about 2.7 t (3 US t, 2.7 UK t)
Diet: meat, including plant–eating dinosaurs
Location: North America (Canada, USA)

Albertosaurus
(al-BER-tuh-SAWR-us)

Allosaurus
(AL-o-SAWR-us)

Meaning of name: different lizard
Lived: 150–140 million years ago
Period: Jurassic
Length: up to 12 m (40 ft)
Weight: up to 5 t (5.5 US t, 4.9 UK t)
Diet: meat, including giant plant-eating dinosaurs!
Location: Africa (Tanzania), North America (USA), Europe (Portugal)

DINO-JOKE

What is noisier than a dinosaur?

Two dinosaurs!

Anchiornis (AN-kee-OR-nis)

Meaning of name: almost bird
Lived: 160–155 million years ago
Period: Jurassic
Length: about 30 cm (1 ft)
Weight: about 110 g (3.9 oz)
Diet: probably insects
Location: Asia (China)

Apatosaurus (ah-PAT-o-SAWR-us)

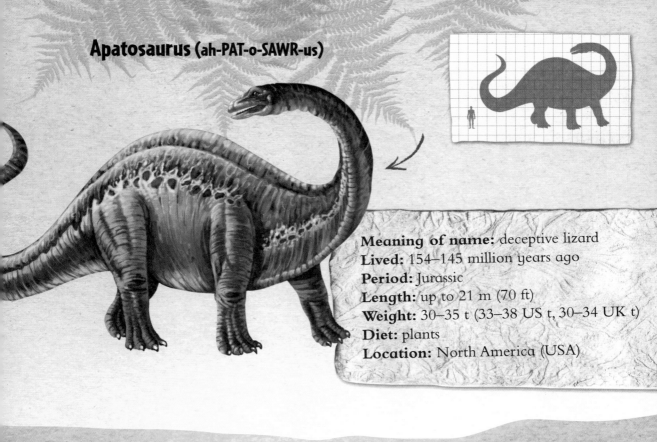

Meaning of name: deceptive lizard
Lived: 154–145 million years ago
Period: Jurassic
Length: up to 21 m (70 ft)
Weight: 30–35 t (33–38 US t, 30–34 UK t)
Diet: plants
Location: North America (USA)

Archaeopteryx
(AHR-kee-OP-ter-iks)

Meaning of name: ancient wing
Lived: 150–147 million years ago
Period: Jurassic
Wingspan: up to 50 cm (1.6 ft)
Weight: up to 500 g (18 oz)
Diet: insects
Location: western Europe (Germany)

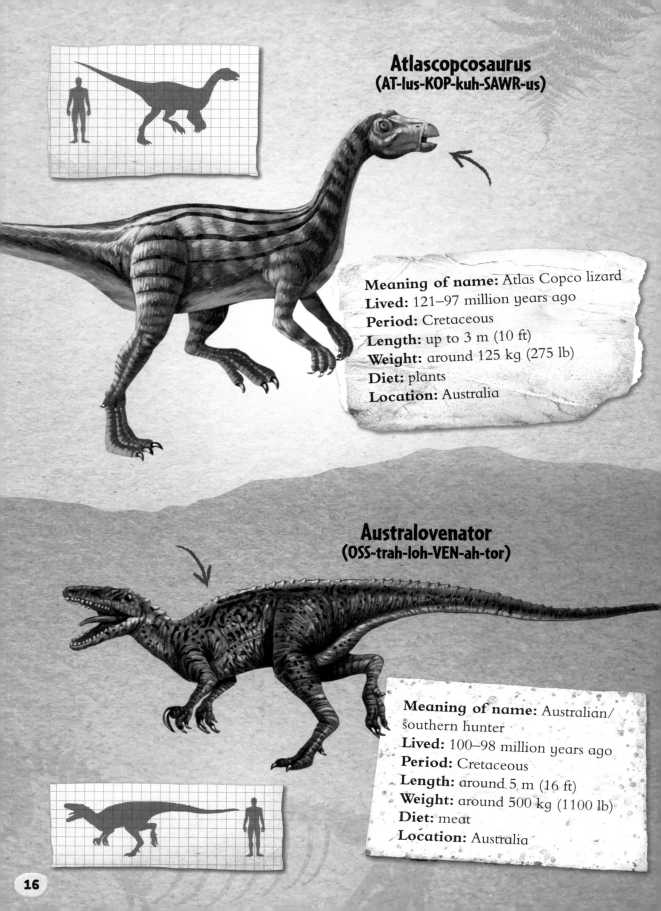

Atlascopcosaurus
(AT-lus-KOP-kuh-SAWR-us)

Meaning of name: Atlas Copco lizard
Lived: 121–97 million years ago
Period: Cretaceous
Length: up to 3 m (10 ft)
Weight: around 125 kg (275 lb)
Diet: plants
Location: Australia

Australovenator
(OSS-trah-loh-VEN-ah-tor)

Meaning of name: Australian/ southern hunter
Lived: 100–98 million years ago
Period: Cretaceous
Length: around 5 m (16 ft)
Weight: around 500 kg (1100 lb)
Diet: meat
Location: Australia

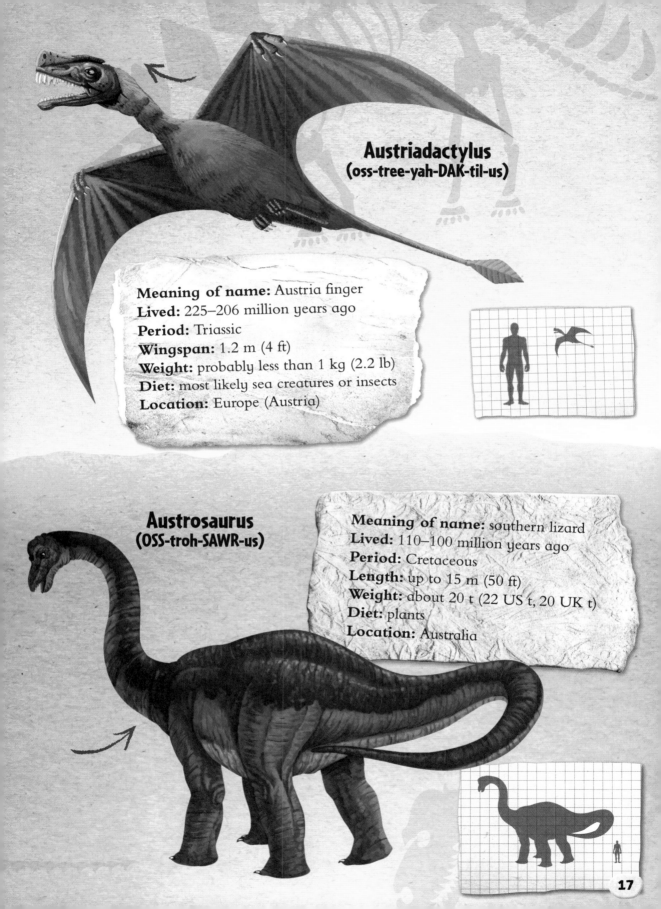

Austriadactylus
(oss-tree-yah-DAK-til-us)

Meaning of name: Austria finger
Lived: 225–206 million years ago
Period: Triassic
Wingspan: 1.2 m (4 ft)
Weight: probably less than 1 kg (2.2 lb)
Diet: most likely sea creatures or insects
Location: Europe (Austria)

Austrosaurus
(OSS-troh-SAWR-us)

Meaning of name: southern lizard
Lived: 110–100 million years ago
Period: Cretaceous
Length: up to 15 m (50 ft)
Weight: about 20 t (22 US t, 20 UK t)
Diet: plants
Location: Australia

Baryonx
(BAR-ee-ON-iks)

Meaning of name: heavy claw
Lived: 130–110 million years ago
Period: Cretaceous
Length: up to 10 m (33 ft)
Weight: about 1.8 t (2 US t, 1.8 UK t)
Diet: meat, including fish
Location: Europe (England and Spain), Africa (Niger)

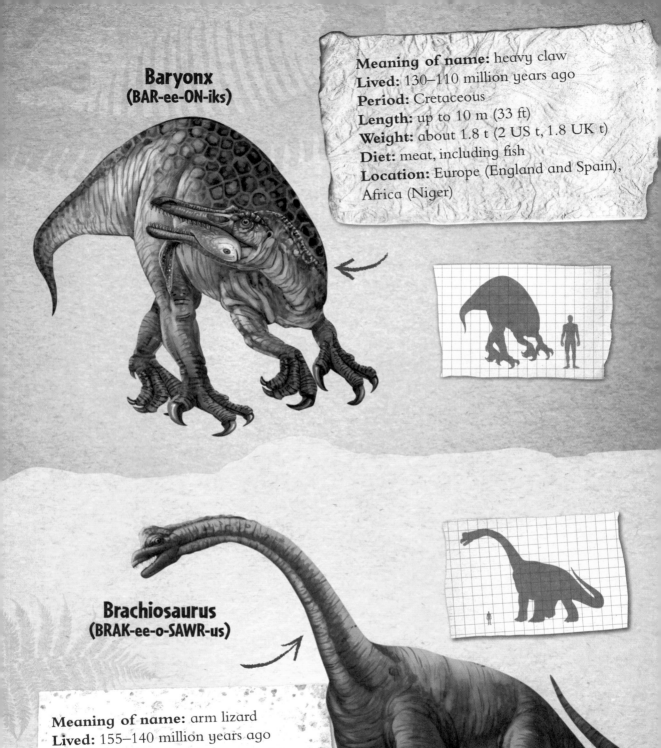

Brachiosaurus
(BRAK-ee-o-SAWR-us)

Meaning of name: arm lizard
Lived: 155–140 million years ago
Period: Jurassic
Length: up to 30 m (100 ft)
Weight: about 54 t (60 US t, 54 UK t)
Diet: plants
Location: North America (USA), Africa (Tanzania, Algeria), Europe (Portugal)

Brachytrachelopan (BRAK-e-TRAK-o-LO-pan)

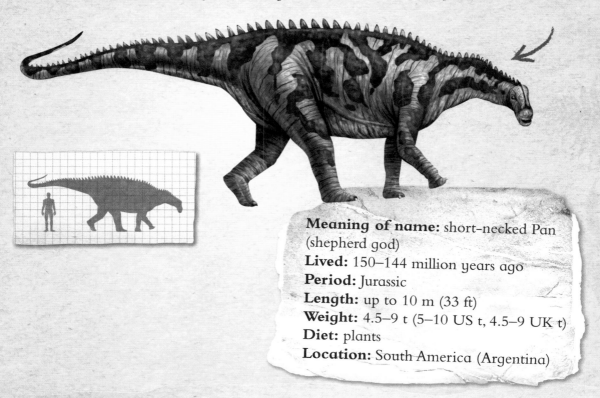

Meaning of name: short-necked Pan (shepherd god)
Lived: 150–144 million years ago
Period: Jurassic
Length: up to 10 m (33 ft)
Weight: 4.5–9 t (5–10 US t, 4.5–9 UK t)
Diet: plants
Location: South America (Argentina)

Camarasaurus (KAM-a-ra-SAWR-us)

Meaning of name: chambered lizard
Lived: 150–140 million years ago
Period: Jurassic
Length: up to 23 m (75 ft)
Weight: around 18 t (20 US t, 18 UK t)
Diet: tough plants
Location: North America (USA)

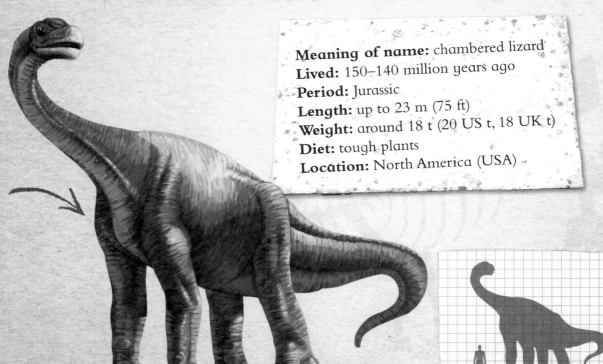

Camelotia (KAM-uh-LOT-ee-uh, also known as Avalonia)

Meaning of name: from Camelot
Lived: 210–205 million years ago
Period: Triassic
Length: up to 9 m (30 ft)
Weight: about 1.8 t (2 US t, 1.8 UK t)
Diet: plants
Location: Europe (England)

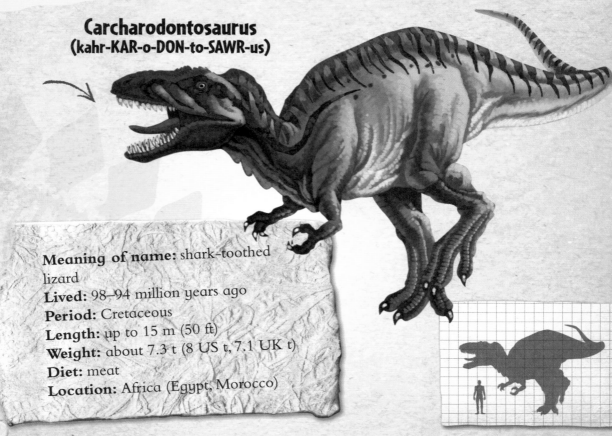

Carcharodontosaurus (kahr-KAR-o-DON-to-SAWR-us)

Meaning of name: shark-toothed lizard
Lived: 98–94 million years ago
Period: Cretaceous
Length: up to 15 m (50 ft)
Weight: about 7.3 t (8 US t, 7.1 UK t)
Diet: meat
Location: Africa (Egypt, Morocco)

Ceratosaurus (se-RAT-o-SAWR-us)

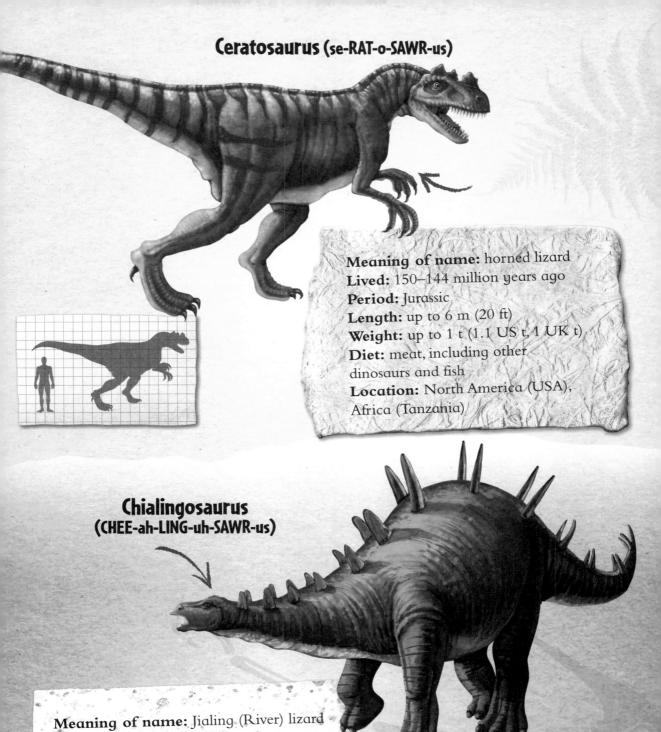

Meaning of name: horned lizard
Lived: 150–144 million years ago
Period: Jurassic
Length: up to 6 m (20 ft)
Weight: up to 1 t (1.1 US t, 1 UK t)
Diet: meat, including other dinosaurs and fish
Location: North America (USA), Africa (Tanzania)

Chialingosaurus (CHEE-ah-LING-uh-SAWR-us)

Meaning of name: Jialing (River) lizard
Lived: 159–142 million years ago
Period: Jurassic
Length: up to 4 m (13 ft)
Weight: 230 kg (500 lb)
Diet: ground plants such as ferns
Location: Asia (China)

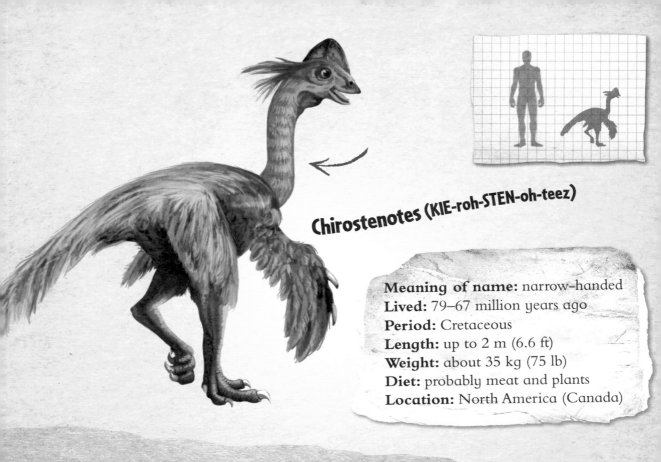

Chirostenotes (KIE-roh-STEN-oh-teez)

Meaning of name: narrow-handed
Lived: 79–67 million years ago
Period: Cretaceous
Length: up to 2 m (6.6 ft)
Weight: about 35 kg (75 lb)
Diet: probably meat and plants
Location: North America (Canada)

Chungkingosaurus (chung-KING-uh-SAWR-us)

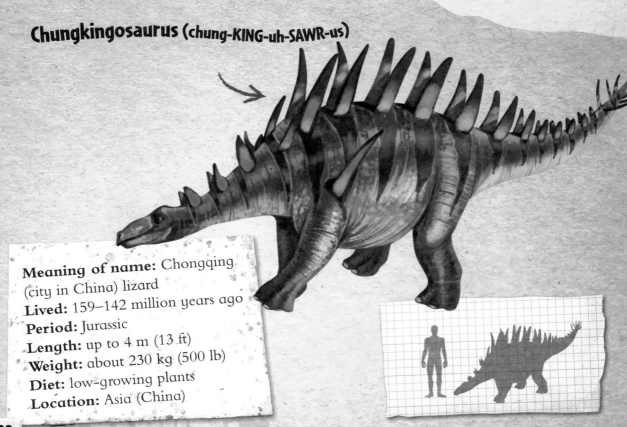

Meaning of name: Chongqing (city in China) lizard
Lived: 159–142 million years ago
Period: Jurassic
Length: up to 4 m (13 ft)
Weight: about 230 kg (500 lb)
Diet: low-growing plants
Location: Asia (China)

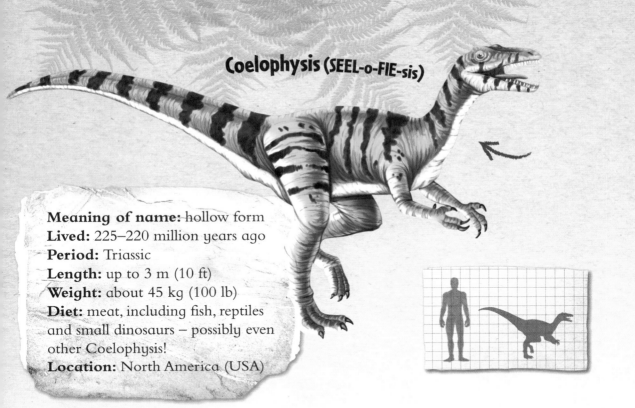

Coelophysis (SEEL-o-FIE-sis)

Meaning of name: hollow form
Lived: 225–220 million years ago
Period: Triassic
Length: up to 3 m (10 ft)
Weight: about 45 kg (100 lb)
Diet: meat, including fish, reptiles and small dinosaurs – possibly even other Coelophysis!
Location: North America (USA)

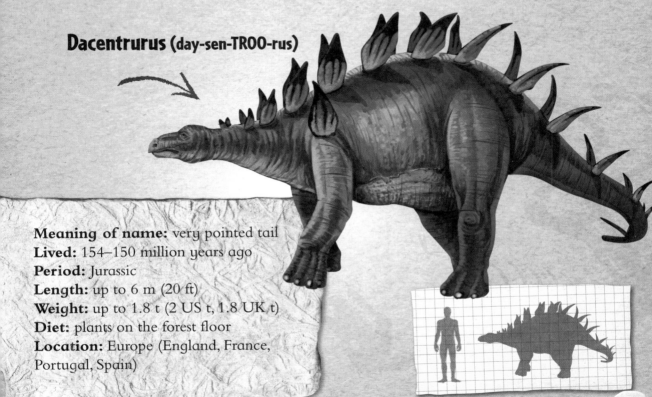

Dacentrurus (day-sen-TROO-rus)

Meaning of name: very pointed tail
Lived: 154–150 million years ago
Period: Jurassic
Length: up to 6 m (20 ft)
Weight: up to 1.8 t (2 US t, 1.8 UK t)
Diet: plants on the forest floor
Location: Europe (England, France, Portugal, Spain)

Deinonychus (die-NON-i-kus)

Meaning of name: terrible claw
Lived: 120–110 million years ago
Period: Cretaceous
Length: up to 3 m (10 ft)
Weight: 80 kg (175 lb)
Diet: meat
Location: North America (USA)

Deltadromeus (DEL-ta-DROHM-ee-us)

Meaning of name: delta runner
Lived: 99–94 million years ago
Period: Cretaceous
Length: about 8 m (26 ft)
Weight: 2.7–3.6 t (3–4 US t, 2.7–3.6 UK t)
Diet: meat
Location: Africa (Morocco)

Diamantinasaurus (dee-uh-man-TEEN-ah-SAWR-us)

Meaning of name: Diamantina (River) lizard
Lived: 100–98 million years ago
Period: Cretaceous
Length: up to 16 m (52 ft)
Weight: 15–20 t (17–22 US t, 15–20 UK t)
Diet: plants
Location: Australia

Dimorphodon (dy-MORE-foh-don)

Meaning of name: two-form tooth
Lived: 175–160 million years ago
Period: Jurassic
Wingspan: about 1.4 m (4.6 ft)
Weight: 2.3 kg (5 lb)
Diet: probably fish or insects
Location: Europe (England), Central America (Mexico)

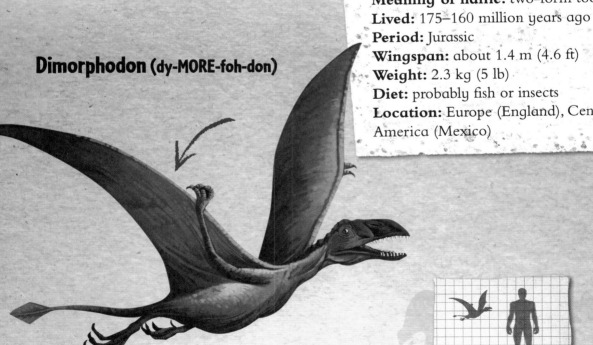

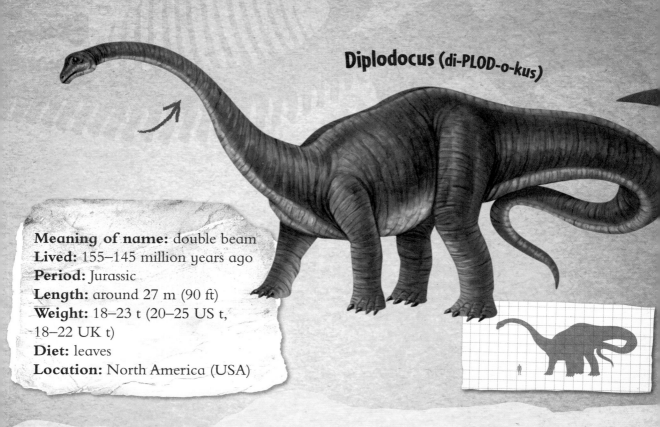

Diplodocus (di-PLOD-o-kus)

Meaning of name: double beam
Lived: 155–145 million years ago
Period: Jurassic
Length: around 27 m (90 ft)
Weight: 18–23 t (20–25 US t,
18–22 UK t)
Diet: leaves
Location: North America (USA)

Meaning of name: Dollo's tooth
Lived: 130–125 million years ago
Period: Cretaceous
Length: up to 6 m (20 ft)
Weight: about 0.9 t (1 US t, 0.9 UK t)
Diet: plants
Location: Europe (Belgium, England)

Dollodon (DOLL-uh-don)

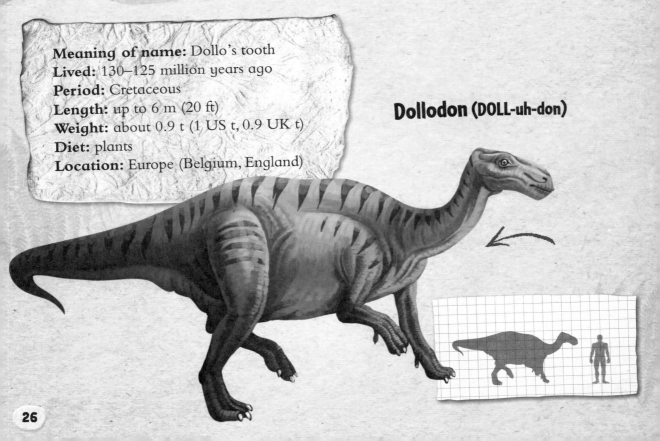

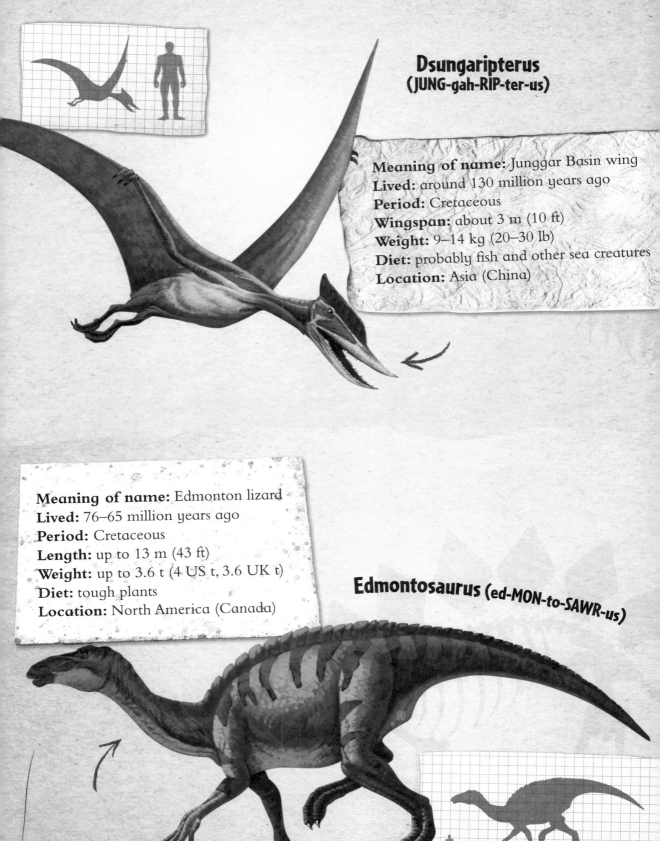

Dsungaripterus
(JUNG-gah-RIP-ter-us)

Meaning of name: Junggar Basin wing
Lived: around 130 million years ago
Period: Cretaceous
Wingspan: about 3 m (10 ft)
Weight: 9–14 kg (20–30 lb)
Diet: probably fish and other sea creatures
Location: Asia (China)

Meaning of name: Edmonton lizard
Lived: 76–65 million years ago
Period: Cretaceous
Length: up to 13 m (43 ft)
Weight: up to 3.6 t (4 US t, 3.6 UK t)
Diet: tough plants
Location: North America (Canada)

Edmontosaurus (ed-MON-to-SAWR-us)

Gargoyleosaurus (gahr-GOY-lo-SAWR-us)

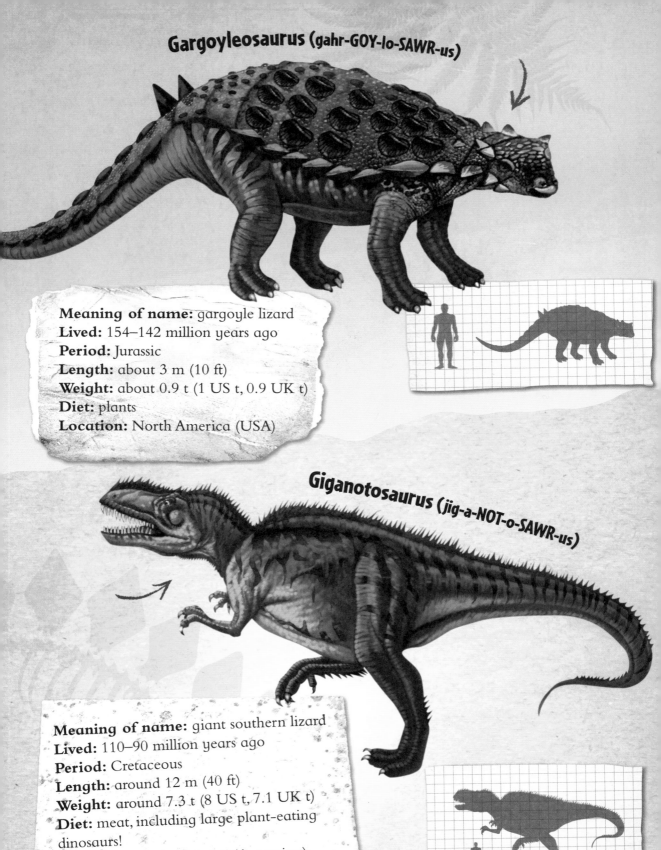

Meaning of name: gargoyle lizard
Lived: 154–142 million years ago
Period: Jurassic
Length: about 3 m (10 ft)
Weight: about 0.9 t (1 US t, 0.9 UK t)
Diet: plants
Location: North America (USA)

Giganotosaurus (jig-a-NOT-o-SAWR-us)

Meaning of name: giant southern lizard
Lived: 110–90 million years ago
Period: Cretaceous
Length: around 12 m (40 ft)
Weight: around 7.3 t (8 US t, 7.1 UK t)
Diet: meat, including large plant-eating dinosaurs!
Location: South America (Argentina)

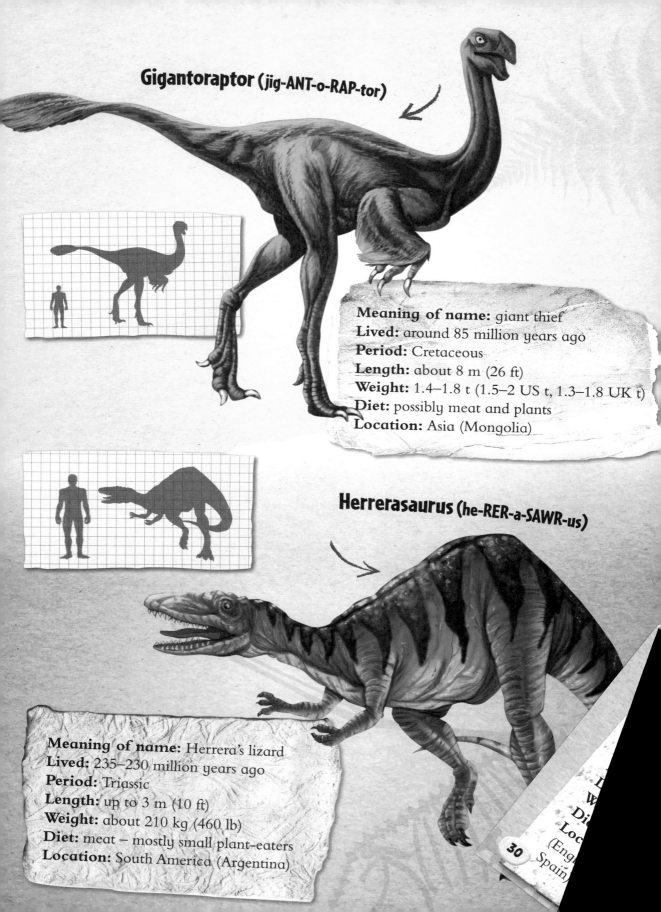

Gigantoraptor (jig-ANT-o-RAP-tor)

Meaning of name: giant thief
Lived: around 85 million years ago
Period: Cretaceous
Length: about 8 m (26 ft)
Weight: 1.4–1.8 t (1.5–2 US t, 1.3–1.8 UK t)
Diet: possibly meat and plants
Location: Asia (Mongolia)

Herrerasaurus (he-RER-a-SAWR-us)

Meaning of name: Herrera's lizard
Lived: 235–230 million years ago
Period: Triassic
Length: up to 3 m (10 ft)
Weight: about 210 kg (460 lb)
Diet: meat – mostly small plant-eaters
Location: South America (Argentina)

Hypacrosaurus
(high-PACK-roh-SAWR-us)

Meaning of name: nearly the highest lizard
Lived: 75–70 million years ago
Period: Cretaceous
Length: about 9 m (30 ft)
Weight: about 4 t (4.4 US t, 3.9 UK t)
Diet: plants
Location: North America (Canada, USA)

Iguanodon (i-GWAHN-o-don)

Meaning of name: iguana tooth
Lived: 140–110 million years ago
Period: Cretaceous
Length/height: up to 10 m (33 ft)
Weight: about 4.5 t (5 US t, 4.5 UK t)
Diet: plants
Location: North America (USA), Europe
(England, France, Germany, Belgium,
Spain), Asia (Mongolia)

Jobaria (jo-BAR-ee-a)

Meaning of name: Jobar
(a mythical animal)
Lived: about 135 million years ago
Period: Cretaceous
Length: up to 21 m (70 ft)
Weight: about 18 t (20 US t, 18 UK t)
Diet: plants
Location: Africa (Niger)

Kentrosaurus (KEN-tro-SAWR-us)

Meaning of name: spiky lizard
Lived: 155–150 million years ago
Period: Jurassic
Length: up to 5 m (16 ft)
Weight: 1.8 t (2 US t, 1.8 UK t)
Diet: low-growing plants
Location: Africa (Tanzania)

Lapparentosaurus
(LA-pah-REN-tuh-SAWR-us)

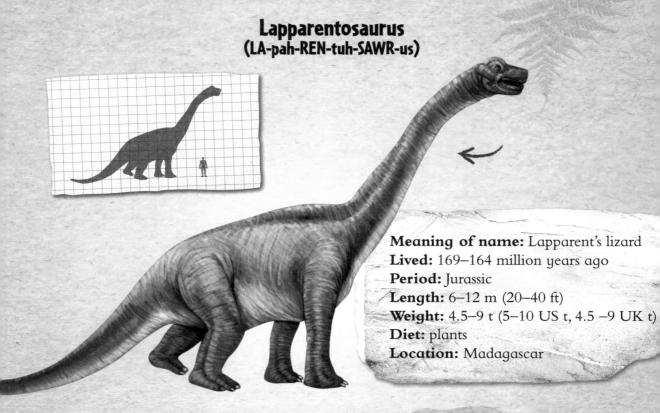

Meaning of name: Lapparent's lizard
Lived: 169–164 million years ago
Period: Jurassic
Length: 6–12 m (20–40 ft)
Weight: 4.5–9 t (5–10 US t, 4.5 –9 UK t)
Diet: plants
Location: Madagascar

Liliensternus (LIL-ee-en-SHTER-nus)

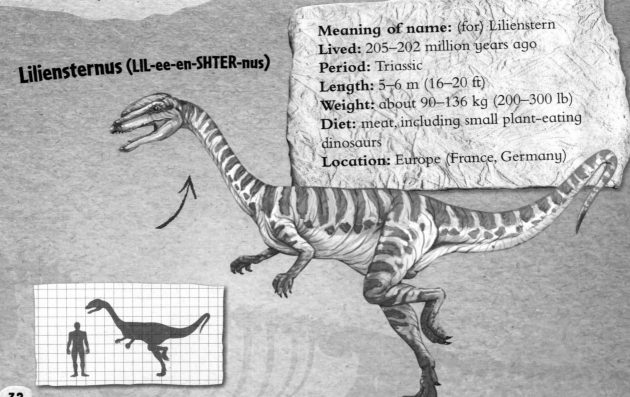

Meaning of name: (for) Lilienstern
Lived: 205–202 million years ago
Period: Triassic
Length: 5–6 m (16–20 ft)
Weight: about 90–136 kg (200–300 lb)
Diet: meat, including small plant-eating dinosaurs
Location: Europe (France, Germany)

Lurdusaurus (LOR-duh-SAWR-us)

Meaning of name: heavy lizard
Lived: 120–110 million years ago
Period: Cretaceous
Length: up to 9 m (30 ft)
Weight: about 5.4 t (6 US t, 5.4 UK t)
Diet: plants
Location: Africa (Niger)

**Massospondylus
(ma-so-SPON-di-lus)**

Meaning of name: large vertebrae
Lived: 208–194 million years ago
Period: Jurassic
Length: about 4 m (13 ft)
Weight: about 140 kg (300 lb)
Diet: plants
Location: Africa (Lesotho, Zimbabwe, South Africa), North America (USA)

Megalosaurus (MEG-a-lo-SAWR-us)

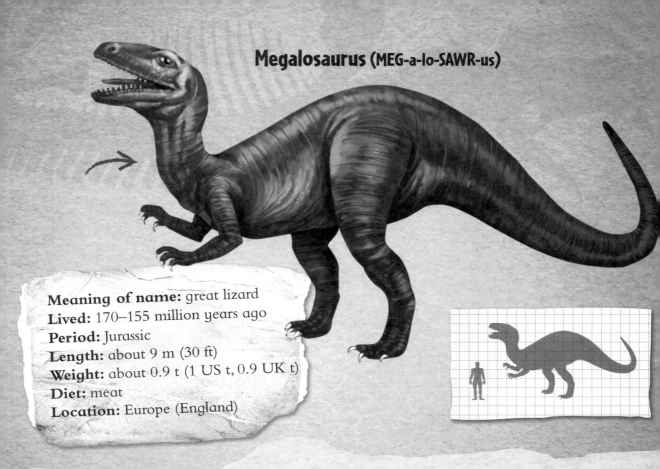

Meaning of name: great lizard
Lived: 170–155 million years ago
Period: Jurassic
Length: about 9 m (30 ft)
Weight: about 0.9 t (1 US t, 0.9 UK t)
Diet: meat
Location: Europe (England)

Melanorosaurus
(mel-uh-NOR-uh-SAWR-us)

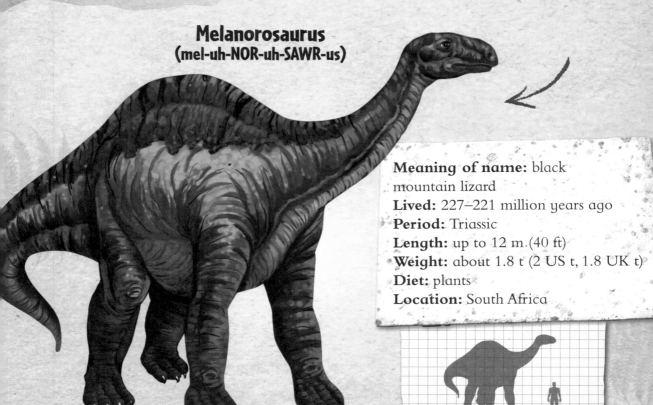

Meaning of name: black mountain lizard
Lived: 227–221 million years ago
Period: Triassic
Length: up to 12 m (40 ft)
Weight: about 1.8 t (2 US t, 1.8 UK t)
Diet: plants
Location: South Africa

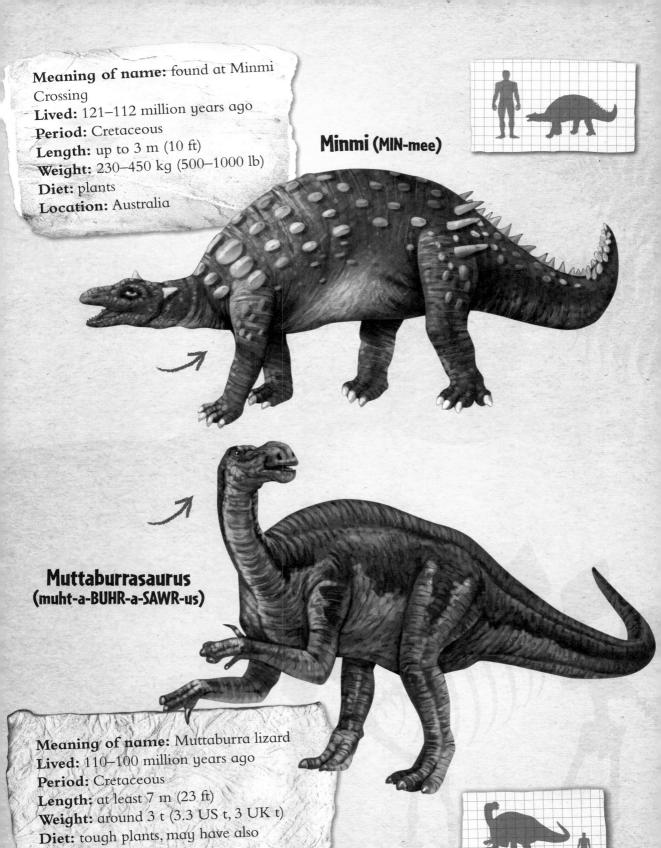

Meaning of name: found at Minmi
Crossing
Lived: 121–112 million years ago
Period: Cretaceous
Length: up to 3 m (10 ft)
Weight: 230–450 kg (500–1000 lb)
Diet: plants
Location: Australia

Minmi (MIN-mee)

Muttaburrasaurus
(muht-a-BUHR-a-SAWR-us)

Meaning of name: Muttaburra lizard
Lived: 110–100 million years ago
Period: Cretaceous
Length: at least 7 m (23 ft)
Weight: around 3 t (3.3 US t, 3 UK t)
Diet: tough plants, may have also
eaten some meat
Location: Australia

Olorotitan (oh-LOH-roh-tie-tan)

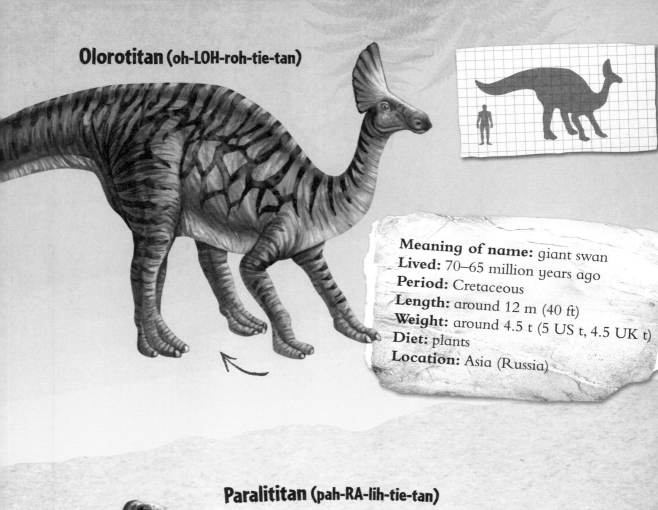

Meaning of name: giant swan
Lived: 70–65 million years ago
Period: Cretaceous
Length: around 12 m (40 ft)
Weight: around 4.5 t (5 US t, 4.5 UK t)
Diet: plants
Location: Asia (Russia)

Paralititan (pah-RA-lih-tie-tan)

Meaning of name: tidal giant
Lived: 99–94 million years ago
Period: Cretaceous
Length: 28–30 m (90–100 ft)
Weight: about 70 t (77 US t, 69 UK t)
Diet: plants
Location: Africa (Egypt)

Meaning of name: like Saurolophus (crested lizard)
Lived: 76–74 million years ago
Period: Cretaceous
Length: up to 11 m (36 ft)
Weight: about 3.6 t (4 US t, 3.6 UK t)
Diet: plants, including pine needles, leaves and twigs
Location: North America (Canada, USA)

Parasaurolophus
(PAR-a-saw-ROL-o-fus)

Pisanosaurus
(pee-SAHN-o-SAWR-us)

Meaning of name: Pisano's lizard
Lived: 227–221 million years ago
Period: Triassic
Length: up to 90 cm (3 ft)
Weight: about 7 kg (15 lb)
Diet: plants
Location: South America (Argentina)

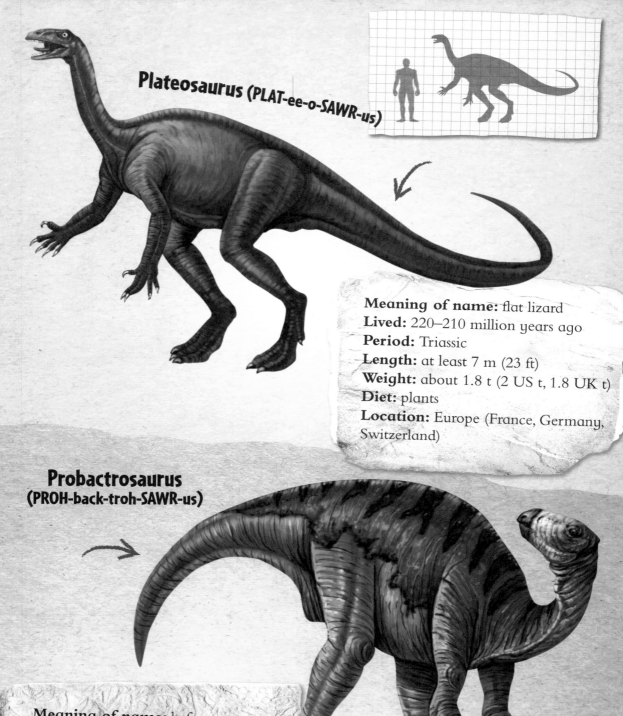

Plateosaurus (PLAT-ee-o-SAWR-us)

Meaning of name: flat lizard
Lived: 220–210 million years ago
Period: Triassic
Length: at least 7 m (23 ft)
Weight: about 1.8 t (2 US t, 1.8 UK t)
Diet: plants
Location: Europe (France, Germany, Switzerland)

Probactrosaurus
(PROH-back-troh-SAWR-us)

Meaning of name: before Bactrosaurus
Lived: 110–100 million years ago
Period: Cretaceous
Length: up to 6 m (20 ft)
Weight: about 0.9 t (1 US t, 0.9 UK t)
Diet: plants
Location: Asia (China)

Protoceratops (PROH-to-SER-a-tops)

Meaning of name: first horned face
Lived: 85–80 million years ago
Period: Cretaceous
Length: up to 1.8 m (6 ft)
Weight: about 180 kg (400 lb)
Diet: low-growing plants
Location: Asia (China, Mongolia)

Pteranodon (TER-an-oh-don)

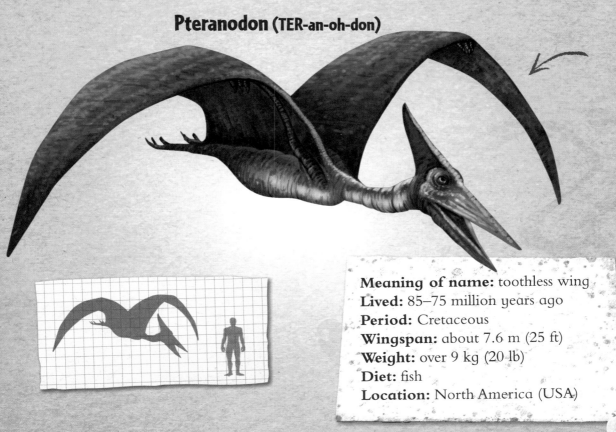

Meaning of name: toothless wing
Lived: 85–75 million years ago
Period: Cretaceous
Wingspan: about 7.6 m (25 ft)
Weight: over 9 kg (20 lb)
Diet: fish
Location: North America (USA)

Quetzalcoatlus (KWET-zal-ko-AT-lus)

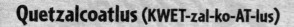

Meaning of name: after Quetzalcoatl (Aztec god)
Lived: 70–65 million years ago
Period: Cretaceous
Wingspan: around 12 m (40 ft)
Weight: around 100 kg (220 lb)
Diet: meat, including fish and other sea creatures
Location: North America (USA)

Rhabdodon (RAB-doh-don)

Meaning of name: rod tooth
Lived: 76–70 million years ago
Period: Cretaceous
Length: up to 4 m (13 ft)
Weight: 115–230 kg (250–500 lb)
Diet: plants
Location: Europe (Austria, France, Spain, Romania)

Rinconsaurus (RIN-kon-SAWR-us)

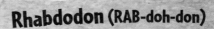

Meaning of name: lizard found at Rincón de los Sauces
Lived: 99–65 million years ago
Period: Cretaceous
Length: up to 14 m (46 ft)
Weight: up to 12 t (13 US t, 12 UK t)
Diet: plants
Location: South America (Argentina)

Saichania (sie-KAHN-ee-a)

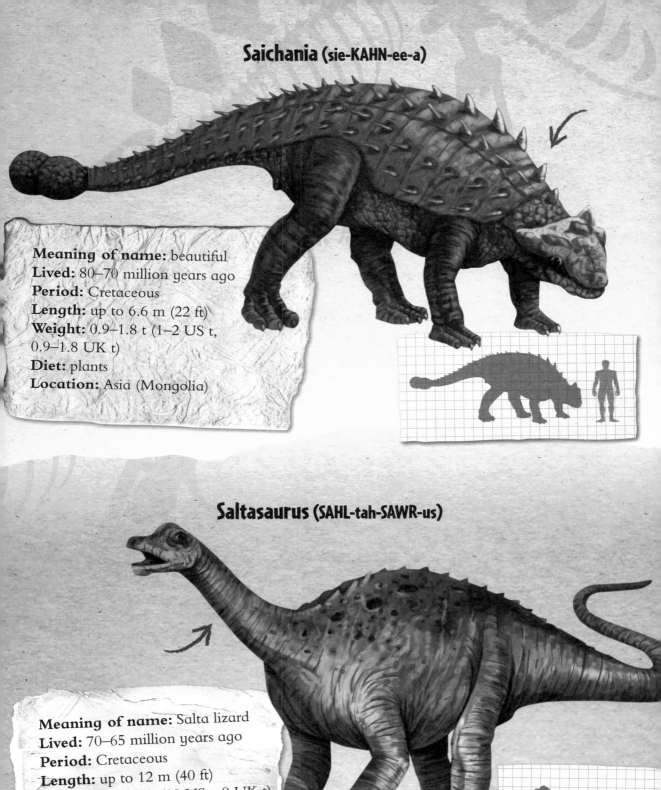

Meaning of name: beautiful
Lived: 80–70 million years ago
Period: Cretaceous
Length: up to 6.6 m (22 ft)
Weight: 0.9–1.8 t (1–2 US t,
0.9–1.8 UK t)
Diet: plants
Location: Asia (Mongolia)

Saltasaurus (SAHL-tah-SAWR-us)

Meaning of name: Salta lizard
Lived: 70–65 million years ago
Period: Cretaceous
Length: up to 12 m (40 ft)
Weight: up to 9 t (10 US t, 9 UK t)
Diet: plants
Location: South America
(Argentina, Uruguay)

Spinosaurus (SPIE-no-SAWR-us)

Meaning of name: thorn lizard
Lived: 95–70 million years ago
Period: Cretaceous
Length: up to 18 m (60 ft)
Weight: about 6.4 t (7 US t, 6.3 UK t)
Diet: meat, including other dinosaurs and large fish
Location: Africa (Egypt, Morocco)

Stegosaurus (STEG-o-SAWR-us)

Meaning of name: roof lizard
Lived: 155–144 million years ago
Period: Jurassic
Length: up to 9 m (30 ft)
Weight: about 2.7 t (3 US t, 2.7 UK t)
Diet: low-growing plants
Location: North America (USA)

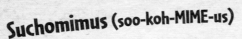

Suchomimus (soo-koh-MIME-us)

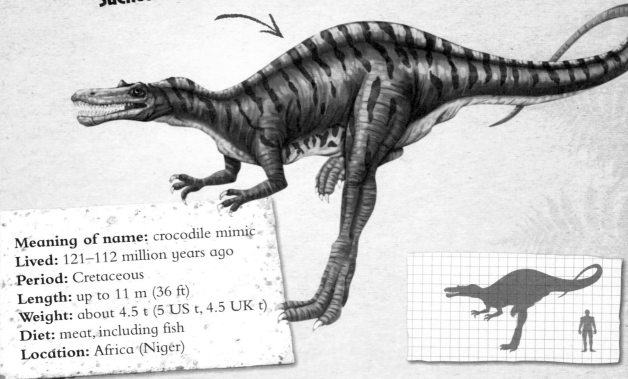

Meaning of name: crocodile mimic
Lived: 121–112 million years ago
Period: Cretaceous
Length: up to 11 m (36 ft)
Weight: about 4.5 t (5 US t, 4.5 UK t)
Diet: meat, including fish
Location: Africa (Niger)

Telmatosaurus (TEL-ma-to-SAWR-us)

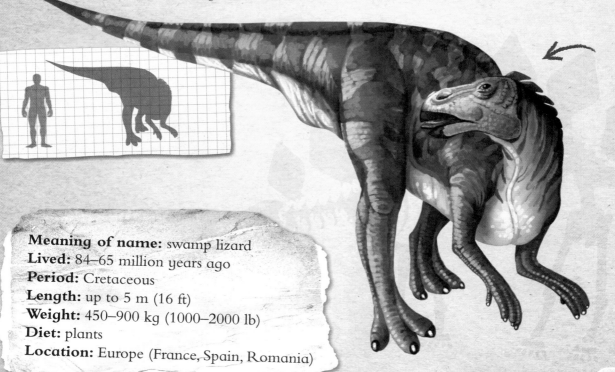

Meaning of name: swamp lizard
Lived: 84–65 million years ago
Period: Cretaceous
Length: up to 5 m (16 ft)
Weight: 450–900 kg (1000–2000 lb)
Diet: plants
Location: Europe (France, Spain, Romania)

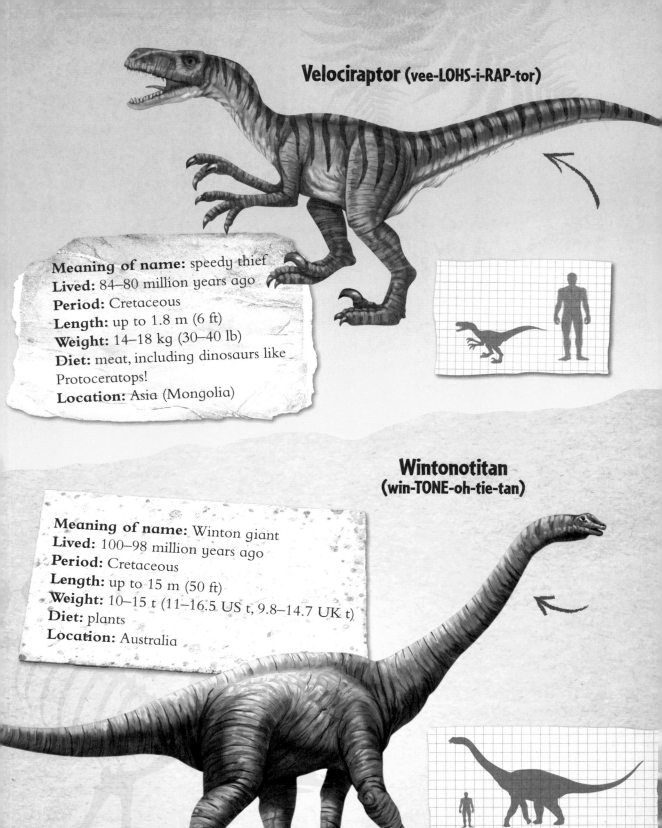

Velociraptor (vee-LOHS-i-RAP-tor)

Meaning of name: speedy thief
Lived: 84–80 million years ago
Period: Cretaceous
Length: up to 1.8 m (6 ft)
Weight: 14–18 kg (30–40 lb)
Diet: meat, including dinosaurs like Protoceratops!
Location: Asia (Mongolia)

Wintonotitan (win-TONE-oh-tie-tan)

Meaning of name: Winton giant
Lived: 100–98 million years ago
Period: Cretaceous
Length: up to 15 m (50 ft)
Weight: 10–15 t (11–16.5 US t, 9.8–14.7 UK t)
Diet: plants
Location: Australia

Yangchuanosaurus
(YAHNG-chwahn-o-SAWR-us)

Meaning of name: Yangchuan lizard
Lived: 160–144 million years ago
Period: Jurassic
Length: up to 10 m (33 ft)
Weight: about 2.4 t (2,6 US t, 2.3 UK t)
Diet: meat
Location: Asia (China)

Zalmoxes (zal-MOCK-sees)

Meaning of name: Zalmoxes
(an ancient god)
Lived: 70–65 million years ago
Period: Cretaceous
Length: up to 4.5 m (15 ft)
Weight: about 230 kg (500 lb)
Diet: plants
Location: Europe (Romania)

DINOSAUR

NORTH AMERICA

EUROPE

SOUTH AMERICA

AFRICA

Chirostenotes (Jurassic)

Triceratops (Cretaceous)

Deinonychus (Cretaceous)

Alamosaurus (Cretaceous)

Acrocanthosaurus (Cretaceous)

Apatosaurus (Jurassic)

Camarasaurus (Jurassic)

Coelophysis (Triassic)

Parasaurolophus (Cretaceous)

Ceratosaurus (Jurassic)

Albertosaurus (Cretaceous)

Pteranodon (Cretaceous)

Diplodocus (Jurassic)

Edmontosaurus (Cretaceous)

Hypacrosaurus (Cretaceous)

Stegosaurus (Jurassic)

Gargoyleosaurus (Jurassic)

Tyrannosaurus (Cretaceous)

Quetzalcoatlus (Cretaceous)

Avalonia (Triassic)

Plateosaurus (Triassic)

Archaeoptery (Jurassic)

Dacentrurus (Jurassic)

Baryonyx (Cretaceous)

Megalosaurus (Jurassic)

Zalmoxes (Cretaceous)

Dollodon (Cretaceous)

Rhabdodon (Cretaceous)

Saltasaurus (Cretaceous)

Unenlagia (Cretaceous)

Brachytrachelopan (Jurassic)

Herrerasaurus (Triassic)

Pisanosaurus (Triassic)

Rinconsaurus (Cretaceous)

Giganotosaurus (Cretaceous)

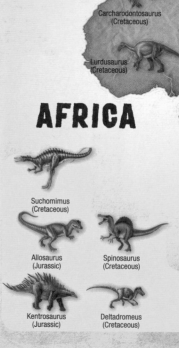

Carcharodontosaurus (Cretaceous)

Lurdusaurus (Cretaceous)

Suchomimus (Cretaceous)

Allosaurus (Jurassic)

Spinosaurus (Cretaceous)

Kentrosaurus (Jurassic)

Deltadromeus (Cretaceous)

Note: This is a representational map, not to scale, and designed for entertainment purposes only.

WORLD MAP

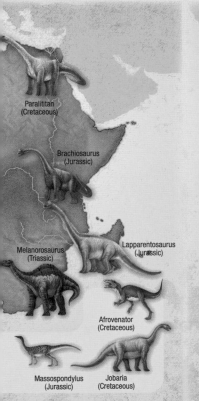

ASIA

OCEANIA

Velociraptor
(Cretaceous)

Olorotitan
(Cretaceous)

Probactrosaurus
(Cretaceous)

Chungkingosaurus
(Jurassic)

Telmatosaurus
(Cretaceous)

Iguanodon
(Cretaceous)

Liliensternus
(Triassic)

Dimorphodon
(Jurassic)

Austriadactylus
(Triassic)

Chialingosaurus
(Jurassic)

Dsungaripterus
(Cretaceous)

Gigantoraptor
(Cretaceous)

Saichania
(Cretaceous)

Protoceratops
(Cretaceous)

Yangchuanosaurus
(Jurassic)

Anchiornis
(Jurassic)

Paralititan
(Cretaceous)

Brachiosaurus
(Jurassic)

Melanorosaurus
(Triassic)

Lapparentosaurus
(Jurassic)

Afrovenator
(Cretaceous)

Massospondylus
(Jurassic)

Jobaria
(Cretaceous)

Minmi
(Cretaceous)

Austrosaurus
(Cretaceous)

Atlascopcosaurus
(Cretaceous)

Muttaburrasaurus
(Cretaceous)

Australovenator
(Cretaceous)

Diamantinasaurus
(Cretaceous)

Wintonotitan
(Cretaceous)

CONCLUSION

Dinosaur fossils have been found all over Earth, and from these fossils we can guess where and when dinosaurs lived. This map of the world is divided into the continents as they are today. Remember, the world was a changing place in the time of the dinosaurs and not all dinosaurs shared the earth at the same time. They lived in these parts of the world during the Triassic, Jurassic and Cretaceous periods.

Dinosaurs left a huge mark on the world and offer so many clues as to how they lived and the different species that roamed the earth. Discoveries are still being made today and will continue for years to come, as more fossils and facts emerge about these amazing creatures!

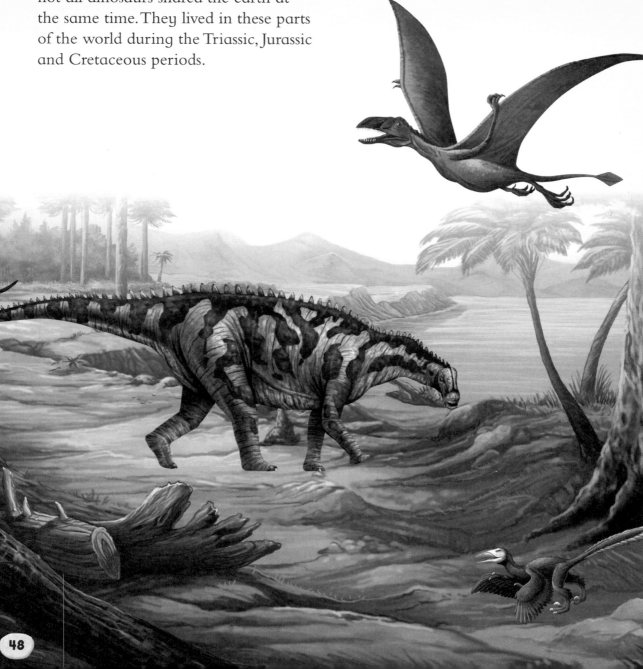